FP  TO CALMER WATERS

Sailor At Sea, Salesman Ashore

*'Some went down to the sea in ships,
doing business in great waters'. Psalm 107*

With best Wishes

Tony Teare.

FROM STORMY SEAS TO CALMER WATERS

Sailor At Sea, Salesman Ashore

Commander Anthony Pearse

BREWIN BOOKS

First published by
Brewin Books Ltd, 56 Alcester Road,
Studley, Warwickshire B80 7LG in 2008
www.brewinbooks.com

ISBN: 978-1-85858-427-0

A Cataloguing in Publication Record
for this title is available from the British Library

Typeset in Stempel Garamond
Printed in Great Britain by
The Alden Press

FROM STORMY SEAS TO CALMER WATERS

Sailor At Sea, Salesman Ashore

HOVE, CHATHAM, GREENWICH

To those not connected by family or friends also in the same profession, one can believe that their idea of a life of a serviceman is that he wears his uniform with pride, is prepared to defend Queen and country and, when necessary and probably against his will, go to war. On the converse, he will travel and play lots of sport. Rather dull and unimaginative perhaps, and, to many not so fortunate, a fairly accurate description.

I consider myself a middle of the road sort of bloke, not out to set the world alight and with no special privileges. Nevertheless I do consider myself, when I look back on my service and later years, both fortunate and lucky having led a life full, varied and interesting. I suspect that most of my ilk would mirror my experience. The slogan "Jack of all trades and Master of none" could well be attached. But so often fresh blood and original thought can breathe new and invigorating life into what had become an intractable problem.

What follows is, as near as my octogenarian memory will allow, a chronological record of my 37 years as a naval officer, and an equally challenging time in commerce. Whilst there have been many changes since my retirement from the navy, I honestly believe the services still offer a challenging and rewarding career.

At the age of 13, I was despatched, for my Secondary School training, to The Nautical College Pangbourne. Not, I think, that my parents or I, realised that I was destined for the

The author aged 13.

sea – and nor did we live near it – but only that I had shown certain interest in that direction. Unlike the naval college at Dartmouth, a large proportion of the students at Pangbourne found their careers in other directions.

By the end of 1941, two years after the start of the war, no further decisions were required by me and I found myself, at just 18 years of age, a Temporary, Probationary, Midshipman Royal Naval Reserve – in naval parlance, the lowest form of animal life. By this time I had decided on my career and in normal times would then have proceeded to The Royal Naval College Dartmouth from which I, (hopefully), would have emerged as a career Midshipman. I vowed that, somehow, I would have the Reserve eradicated.

After a hectic and scarcely sufficient basic training at Hove to learn how to march; at Chatham to learn the rudimentary rules of naval life; and to The Royal Naval College at Greenwich to learn how to eat with a knife and fork, we were rated suitable to join the fleet. Many who may read this, will have visited the lovely Greenwich college with its beautiful buildings and dramatic Painted Hall. Perhaps we were too young to fully appreciate it but certainly not to "enjoy" nightly raids on London. The young gentlemen, given the task of firewatching on the roof, had to clamber from the ground floor to the second. On their way they passed, on the stairs, the many glamorous young ladies training to be Wren Officers, as they disappeared from the first to the basement., usually in their night attire. I cannot vouch for this, but it was accepted knowledge that the roll call in both areas was not always complete.

USA. INDIAN OCEAN

On our final day of this three month whirl, came the news we were all so eagerly awaiting. Was I to sit behind a desk handing out forms to new recruits; was I to be given flying training; was I to find myself on the North Sea in a grubby minesweeper? Unbelievably, and beyond my wildest dreams, I was commanded by The Lords Commissioners of the Admiralty to repair to one of the most famous battleships in the Royal Navy, HMS WARSPITE. NOW I was in the navy!

Secrecy in wartime is paramount and considerable research was to be needed before I could find out where I could carry out my orders. Not Portsmouth nor Plymouth nor Rosyth but in a place for which I needed a map, Seattle in Washington BC, USA.

Poor old WARSPITE had been in the thick of it during the battles for Crete and she had been severely mauled. Refitting in British shipyards was not for the fainthearted with so many of the ports flattened. Whilst America had then

HMS Warspite. Photograph courtesy of the Imperial War Museum, London. FL22120.

not joined the war, there was nothing to stop her assisting one of her friends and, accordingly, WARSPITE was despatched to the safety of Bremerton Navy Shipyard, Seattle to patch up her wounds.

On a cold and dreary day, another Midshipman and I found ourselves in Mersey Docks Liverpool, standing on the deck of an old eight knot rusty freighter, SS PORT SYDNEY, bound for Halifax Nova Scotia. And two days later, with a feeling of depression greater than that which had brought the violent gale, we were plunging up and down as if controlled by a string, shipping green water from mountainous seas. Of the other 23 ships of the original convoy, there was no sign. Very few slow ships sailing alone escaped the roaming wolf packs of submarines and our thoughts, homesickness and fear of the unknown made us silent and morose shipmates. It is believed that poor old PORT SYDNEY lasted two more trips. How many of the crew I knew so well perished with her?

By the time land was sighted, the two young men were swaggering, cocky young bloods; seen it all and survived. But, just to make sure we knew our station, no-one bothered to tell us that, due to the weather and other considerations, this was not Halifax Nova Scotia but Baltimore Maryland, very much further south.

Although America was now firmly in the war, lights were on; food was plenty; we were in full uniform; girls were in abundance; senior officers were far away. Bliss.

A quick look at the map and we realised that to get north to Montreal to catch the cross Canada railway from which outfit His Majesty had obtained our tickets, was going to necessitate passing through New York. And further enquiries informed us that, it now being on the verge of New Years Eve, the trains were pretty busy. Being young, resourceful, and I suppose slightly irresponsible, this setback did not deter us and we settled back to enjoy an unforgettable New Years Eve in the vibrant big city.

Of course we did not realise until much later, but two things slightly marred this idyllic four days. First that we were to be late joining our first ship and, second, that some kind soul sent my dear Mother a copy of a magazine in which there was a long article on the British at war in USA and where there were pictures of self standing on the bar of The Astor Hotel singing "she had to go and lose it at the Astor, it was the only one she ever had," and of two young Midshipmen, coats undone and hatless but otherwise in uniform, leading a Conga round Times Square. I trust that I have never been one to complain about the antics of modern youth.

All good things come to an end or nearly so, and at last we were on board a train to take one of the most beautiful four day train journeys to be had. Through the Winnipeg Plains and up the Rocky Mountains making a stop at the delightfully named Oshkosh, and finally sweeping into the exotic city of Vancouver.

By now it was hardly a surprise to be told that the great ship had left Seattle and was somewhere in Qualicom Sound, not far from Vancouver, doing her post refit trials.

The Duke of Sutherland's ex yacht SANS SPUR, had been requisitioned as a small inshore patrol craft and off we went, in a driving snowstorm and with no visibility, to search for our prize. Suddenly an enormous hulk emerged out of the gloom, stopped, lowered a ladder over the side to allow two sheepish gentlemen to clamber aboard. One small part of our basic training had impressed on us the custom of saluting the quarterdeck at such a moment. This we did – secretly rather pleased to be welcomed by someone with gold braid on his arm from elbow to cuff – only to be brought back to earth with the words shouted at us: "YOU ARE LATE". And so began my long and affectionate love affair with this dear old lady, so titled a year back when ordered by the Commander In Chief Mediterranean to proceed with all despatch to a certain area, and who expressed his pleasure with a signal stating that "the dear old lady could still pick up her skirts and run".

It must be impressed here, that the author had paid his only visit to a warship when, as a small cadet, he had attended the Naval Review in 1937. The shock and bewilderment of standing on a 35000 ton majestic vessel, the home of over 1300 souls, many miles from loved ones from which there had been little contact for a considerable time, produced a lump in the throat which, so disastrously, nearly welled up into tears. And worse was to come when confronted with the rest of the young Midshipmen, having been aboard all of two months and thus, experienced and hardened sailors, and who proceeded to view these newcomers with disdain. I could have been one of the unfortunates in 'Tom Brown's Schooldays'.

The life of a Midshipman is, indeed, strange. An Officer to be trained and sometimes bullied, by his superiors. And an Officer to be trained and shouted at by his underlings but always with each bark, a respectful Sir at the end of a tirade. And at the same time, these tough and hardened sailors managing to imply a feeling of sympathy.

By far the worst treatment was to be had, sometimes, by one's peers. The remainder of the young gentleman (snotties for short) had been onboard for all of two months and there was nothing they did not know.

Duties were many and varied but the task of Midshipman of the Watch., the most varied and exciting but full of traps. The writing up of the Deck Log (narrative of the four hour watch); the supervision of the lookouts and, without doubt the most important especially in the days of bridges open to the elements, the supply of cocoa or 'kye' to the Officer of The Watch, Navigator and, above all, the Captain. In a little cubby hole are kept mugs, cocoa, milk and sugar, together with instructions from your predecessor, as to the preferences of your various masters. Written clearly for my perusal were the words THE CAPTAIN LIKES UNLIMITED SUGAR.

It must be remembered that this was my first night onboard, my first visit to the bridge, my first duty as Midshipman of The Watch and my first meeting with the Captain. At the hour at which the great man wished to be called, I was to be found by his bed shouting in a loud voice CAPTAIN SIR, 0400, Never NEVER place your hands on the body to shake him awake as allegations of assault can result.

A proud man was I, as my God appeared, holding out his hand for his drink so carefully prepared but who was then promptly nearly sick. Just as a joke mind you, but my predecessor from whom I had received a detailed handover, had calmly substituted salt for sugar. Severe punishment for insolence resulted; I learnt my first adult lesson in man's inhumanity to man; and the Midshipman concerned become one of my great friends!

A major refit to a warship entails destruction on a big scale and it is necessary to test in detail, that all has been put back correctly. Post refit trials involve, therefore, detailed investigations into refitted equipment, training on that which is new and a general work up of a large number of souls into a cohesive fighting machine. This can require some weeks but, after several days on the seas around Vancouver and Qualicom Sound, we were pronounced fit to proceed.

The United States had their hands more than full in the Pacific area but the Japanese were still very much in evidence further west in the Indian Ocean. The battleships PRINCE OF WALES and REPULSE, the cruisers DORSETSHIRE and CORNWALL had already been sunk and the aircraft carrier HERMES was soon to follow. To demonstrate the concern showed as to the threat, the Eastern Fleet as it was named, comprised four R Class battleships, three Fleet Aircraft Carriers, several cruisers and a large number of destroyers – a sizeable force. We in WARSPITE were to add further weight.

After a long passage down the American west coast, across to Australia (a short and welcome stop in Sydney), a circuitous tour of the great southern continent and finally a triumphant entry into Trincomalee, Ceylon (Sri Lanka).

The Midshipman's 'flat' in a ship the size of a battleship, is a virtually empty space which could normally accommodate some 20 beds. Instead of such luxury, one is faced with a series of hooks on to each end of which is tied the ends of a hammock. With 35 Midshipmen onboard this space was somewhat crowded and when we approached the tropics I set about finding myself a quiet spot on deck upon which I could place my blanket. You learn fast and I was soon to understand why this luxury was scorned when, at 0530 in the morning, me and my bedding were floating gently as the morning duty watch carried out the timely task of scrubbing decks.

In addition to acting as Midshipman of the Watch, Commanders' 'doggie' or slave, painting ship, driving the ship's boats when in harbour, and being taught, taught, taught, the young Gentlemen have to find time to write a Midshipman's journal. This journal is important to the writer being just one more cog in the wheel which, when put together with other attributes, has an effect on his future prospects. Comprising narrative, sketches and observations, it comes, monthly, under the severe inspection of The Snotties Nurse, a more senior officer with the qualities of therapist, psychiatrist, disciplinarian and, teacher, all the while revered, feared and loved in equal measure. When in Sydney, during our long haul to Ceylon, I had been informed 'with authority' that when the famous harbour bridge was built, the two ends overlapped, when joined together, by a minimal amount and vast quantities of ice were used to contract the metal and allow for a perfect marriage. Information of this must surely earn me good marks and into my journal it went. A notation by the Snotties Nurse that the constructors must have been good builders and contractors, showed that he also had a good sense of humour.

Having swallowed most of the territory east of the Malaysian peninsular, the Japanese were not going to be deterred from attempting further conquests and their large carrier force was still very much in existence. It was decided therefore to continue our operations from further west and the two bases used were the dramatically beautiful Addu Atoll in the Maldive Islands (now the popular resort of tourists), and the cavernous and busy port of Mombasa in Kenya. The aim was then to act as a deterrent to further advances west by the enemy, and, at the same time, to escort and protect the very large troop convoys travelling to and from the Antipodean and European theatres of war.

A Midshipman's pay of 5 shillings per day did not, after deductions for mess bills and clothing, allow for more than very occasional visits to the fleshpots. One of these found three of the young gentlemen enjoying the delights of the Galle Face Hotel in Colombo. Those who will have stayed there on holiday, will recollect the calm and essentially colonial atmosphere and so it was, after their swim, that the three were devouring cucumber sandwiches washed down by Earl Grey tea whilst languishing in the comfortable wicker chairs of the lounge, All this to the delicate strains produced from the strings of violins in the hands of three ladies of an indeterminate age in cocktail frocks. Alive to the realities, the sound of very low flying aircraft had the effect of disappearance under the tables of the majority of the clientele. Rising sheepishly, a few minutes later, it was with considerable embarrassment that it was realised that "we'll gather lilacs" had continued without a note having been lost, by the three old dears. Somerset Maugham I think!

The next few months were interspersed with drama, boredom and excitement but, fortunately, little action. To be remembered were the invitation to Government House in Bombay before which my (only) white uniform had been cleaned and pressed at the suggestion of the ADC. I should have expected that payment that would be required and an invoice was duly presented at the pre-dinner reception, by a turbanned flunky holding out a silver tray in front of 50 other guests. Embarrassing at any time but even more so, when I knew my pockets were empty. And then, a thousand or so miles to the west, the two delectable daughters of the Kings Harbour Master at Mombasa, who had to divide carefully their time between 200 young suitors in the fleet. Whether or not I was favoured, I achieved some five or six assignments with the younger, Mary.

In 1942, aircraft carriers did not have the luxury of angled decks which allow a 'go round again' when the arrester wires have been missed; nor were there powerful caterpults shooting heavy aircraft into take off speed within only a few yards. For the take off, sufficient deck space was required, and for landing, cross wires and then a wire barrier prevented a more serious crash with other aircraft parked forward.

Such hazards and considerable losses, were leading to a serious shortage of naval pilots and immediate action was required. What better or easier than to convince the large number of Midshipmen in the Eastern Fleet that to transfer to the Fleet Air Arm would be exciting and rewarding. Accordingly all of us in turn, were to spend two weeks in one or more of the three carriers in order to gain 'flying experience'.

The famous string constructed bi-plane torpedo bomber the SWORDFISH, was embarked in all three of the ships. Behind the pilot stood the observer and behind him the air gunner. Both these intrepid airmen were attached by means of a harness leading to a bolt in the floor and a G string between the legs, With a cockpit open to the elements, it was a weird, and sometimes intoxicating, method of being propelled through the sky. It also provided a perfect view of what your pilot was up to just in front.

My first pilot, a young Australian, had already been awarded the nickname FEARLESS, evidently with good reason. As the time came to return to Mother after our sortie, it became clear to me looking over his shoulder, that, unless we modified our descent, we were likely to end up in the Captain's quarters aft in the ship. A quick correction was made by my man but too late and too high and one by one the arrester wires were passed by the hook dangling below us. In virtual slow motion (the SWORDFISH never travelled very fast), the barrier approached and, a few seconds later, I lay upside down, hanging by my G string and with the deck a few inches from my eyes. In all fairness such an arrival was not uncommon and "bad luck young man, you will forget all about it after your next flight tomorrow", was considered a reasonable statement by those who had seen it all before.

As already explained, take off required the achievement of sufficient speed across the deck to get airborne. The faster the speed of the ship and the greater the wind, the fewer the yards that were required. High speed fighters must, therefore, start at the back and with the poor old SWORDFISH leading the parade.

Swordfish on Carrier Deck.

At dawn the following day the flight deck was full of sleek MARTLETS and SEAFIRES, more ponderous FULMARS and ALBACORES, and, proudly in front, the gallant SWORDFISH. With the sea calm and the engines started, it was a cacophony of sound as I strode to the leading aircraft glancing up, with relief, at the considerably more mature face of today's pilot. At the same time there was a distinct realisation that the bow of the ship and the water beyond, were undeniably close. It was in slow motion that, with brakes off, we rolled gently but surely to the end of security and, with the simple law of physics, landed with a splash. Fortunately my pilot had realised the need to avoid being hit up the backside by the mighty vessel and as she rushed past, so we committed ourselves to the deep. Fast work by the safety destroyer and with our feet barely wet, we were back where we started. I enjoyed my two weeks flying experience but not enough to become a volunteer to help out.

Following the surrender of the French and the division of France into the Free French and the Petainists, it became vital that the large French Fleet and associated bases were not used against the remaining Allies. Winston Churchill personally ordered that the French Fleet should either fight with the Royal Navy or be neutralised in some way, to prevent it from falling into enemy hands. The pro-axis Petain government refused and, clearly with a heavy heart, the order was given to seek and destroy the ships wherever they were based or were to be found. Some of the individual Commanding officers, as will be seen later, took the brave decision to place their vessels under the command of the Royal Navy. And so began the appalling, but necessary, operation to wipe the French Fleet off the map. The largest of these operations was at Mer-El-Kebir in Algeria and further actions continued elsewhere during the coming months. Undoubtedly, in WARSPITE, one of our saddest moments was the 'capture' of Madagascar. This took the form of firing a warning 15" shell on to the beach at Tamatave, killing, we heard later, the small daughter of the local Doctor who had run down to see the ships. War-UGH.

After many months at sea and with few opportunities for relaxation, it was with great excitement that we learnt that we were to proceed to Durban in South Africa, for a minor refit. As we approached the dock entrance, the strains of a beautiful voice floated across the water, the owner of which eventually materialised into a stately woman dressed completely in white and with a

The author next to the statue of Dame Perla Gibson.

megaphone to her lips. This was to be the famous Lady In White, Dame Perla Gibson. Mrs Gibson, a mother of four, had been persuaded by a friend, to sing a welcome to a troopship, aboard which was her son. Such was the success, that she continued with this welcome, and sailors and other servicemen in over 1000 men of war and troopships, and in 350 hospital ships, were able to hear her beautiful voice. The Royal Navy presented a cairn with a bronze plaque in her memory and in 1995, her Majesty Queen Elizabeth unveiled a statue of her which is now viewed by many who pass through the Ocean terminal in the port.

It is not easy to describe the incredible generosity of the people of South Africa during these years. Every single soul of our ship's company of over 1300 were entertained and made welcome by families throughout Natal, and if we were not able to be with our own loved ones at home, then homesickness was pushed into the background. Another Midshipman and I, were to be placed with a family on a farm, Maritsdal, up in The Drakensburg mountains. Today, 63 years later, I have tracked down the daughter in law of the owners and I will be visiting her later in 2007.

In mid 1943 the tide of battle was turning. Rommel had been defeated and North Africa was reclaimed. It was clear that the next step was the invasion of

Maritsdal farm.

mainland Europe, a daunting task which was going to require massive forces. And so we found ourselves making our way through the Straits of Gibraltar and on into Malta harbour. Although articles and documentaries had prepared us, nothing can describe the appalling damage and devastation wrought on this small island and the award of The George Cross was so well deserved. Although the aerial bombardment was now diminishing, not many days passed without an attack, and our regular base became the picturesque harbour of Marsaslokk, well away from Grand Harbour.

In July 1943, the world rejoiced with the news that the allies had landed in Sicily and, although opposition was fierce, within a remarkably short time, the entire island was captured. WARSPITE together with a vast armada, covered the landings and, apart from a few desultory air attacks, was never in any danger. The significance of these landings changed the whole nature of the war, with the Italians realising that all was lost in their area, the sacking and hanging of Mussolini and the signing of a peace treaty. The ultimate steam past and surrender of The Italian Fleet was a sight never to be forgotten.

In mid September the juggernaut moved on, this time to invade the spine of Europe and the landings at Salerno on the Italian mainland, were begun. At first all went well but the Germans had realised the importance of preventing the enemy taking a foothold and, within only a few days, our forces were in danger of being pushed back into the sea.

The value of heavy warships such as WARSPITE in covering landings such as these, is the ability to provide a large amount of fire power from a considerable distance. But it now became clear that something more was required and so this mighty vessel found itself close to the beaches and with little room to manoeuvre, firing her 15" shells over virtually open sights, at the German tanks behind the beachhead. War is not pretty but the carnage achieved can only be imagined.

In addition to the main armament, a battleship of those days carried a further array of 6" guns together with batteries, port and starboard, of 4" anti-aircraft weapons. High above them on either side of the bridge, were fitted two turrets from which these weapons were controlled. Below these turrets or Directors, were stalks which fitted snugly into sleeves and which provided the only visible means of support.

By now I had my foot on the next rung of the ladder and, as a Sub Lieutenant, was given the task of commanding the port Director. The total complement (including myself) of four, did not amount to much, but the importance of the task should not be under-estimated and I was a proud man.

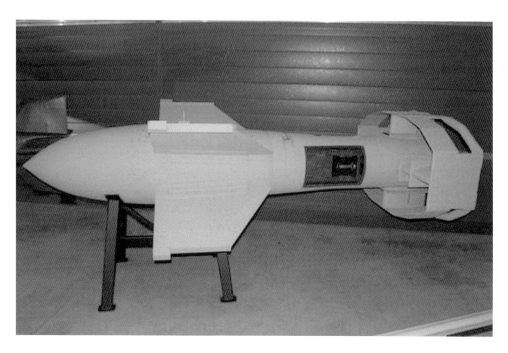

German glider bomb HS293 (Fritz).

As can be imagined, life off the beaches was a busy one and we had become used to, and a bit blasé, about Heinkels and Dorniers so when three more appeared above us and bombs tumbled out of them, I and my little band of men, were not too worried as clearly they were going to miss. However, just in case, I kept my eyes open and, to my, horror, watched as they changed direction and headed for us. With a resounding crump one landed alongside the funnel, twenty feet or so from my eyrie, one near the armour bulge and the third missed astern. My little Director swayed like a daffodil in the breeze but managed, somehow, to stay inside the stalk. This was the first use of the new German glider bomb HS293 or Fritz X and with hits on one battleship (WARSPITE), and two cruisers (SAVANNAH and UGANDA), all within a matter of minutes, there must have been great joy by the Germans in the result.

Unfortunately the direct hit amidships penetrated to the lower decks and in one blow, rendered the mighty warship into a hulk without power – electric or steam. In times of stress, analysis of one's actions is fruitless but I remember with a perfectly clear mind, of my impotence at where I was and the need to place myself where I could be of most use. In fact, of course, it was little more than an act of self preservation. And so, surrounded by smoke, cries and I suppose, temporary panic, I found myself on the quarterdeck, my shoes neatly placed together, life jacket inflated, standing stiffly to attention waiting for the order to abandon ship. How many minutes passed before I realised that all was not quite lost, put on my shoes and regained my dignity, I have absolutely no idea.

The obvious need was to remove this useless but possibly future valuable vessel away from the area before further attacks would send her to the bottom, and the light cruiser EURYALUS was summoned to take us away. Not an easy task as by now, with the weight of sea water onboard, we weighed considerably more than our original displacement. But the tow was passed and slowly we disappeared from the scene and set course for Malta.

In between the land of Italy and Sicily there lie the whirlpools of Scylla and Charybdis and, caught in the whirling maelstrom, the tow was parted and this majestic vessel was left, gyrating slowly but sedately making her way southwards. After what seemed a lifetime but I suppose was really only a few days, we eventually slid between the welcoming breakwaters of Grand Harbour and came to rest heavily bows down.

I have related above, the horrific devastation of this gallant island and what with the state of the dockyard coupled with the enormous weight and draught of the ship, there was simply no way whereby the vessel could be docked. Further delay but eventually four enormous Dutch tugs arrived, grabbed hold of us and thus started the longest, heaviest known tow of the war. Of course our final despatch would have been an enormous success to the enemy and there were few onboard who rated highly our chances of reaching Gibraltar. But the battle still raged in Italy, the Italians had surrendered and the Germans had priorities other than sinking what was already, a pretty useless man of war. And so, much to our relief and surprise, we woke one morning to the sight of the famous Rock and before, too long were snugly alongside the detached mole. At last we could relax.

Not unnaturally, as the water was drained out of the dry dock into which we had eventually been placed, we were all agog to see the seriousness of our damage. But before that was to happen, we were to be sickened by the remains of those killed some months earlier, spewing out of the cavernous hole. May God Rest Their Souls.

When viewed from the bottom of the dock, it became a source of wonder as to why the ship had not broken her back and we admired the strength of her construction. Clearly it was appreciated that her life as a battleship of the fleet had come to an end. But could her guns be used as a platform for bombardment at the landings further north which clearly were on their way? The recoil from the firing of a 15" gun is awesome. Obviously the only way to

HMS Warspite under tow. Photograph courtesy of the Imperial War Museum, London. FL22135.

find out was to fix a mammoth plate over the hole, go to sea and fire a 15inch shell. Just to make sure that a detailed report could be formulated, a young Engineer Officer was to sit on this plate to see whether he would be discharged into the sea. Am not aware if he was a volunteer but he was a very brave man and was rewarded later.

As the big moment arrived my feelings (and I suspect, those of many others) were akin to standing outside the headmaster's study after having committed a grave indiscretion. Or perhaps the imminent visit to a dentist with a tooth destined to be withdrawn. Certainly there was a distinct wish to empty the bladder. But, BANG, a big shudder, a rock to one side and then the other and, finally, calm. All was OK then.

Whether or not this lovely old ship could be used as a bombardment platform at the forthcoming Normandy landings (she was), it was clear that she was in no state to sail home alone and would have to wait for a suitable convoy. Personnel were too valuable to leave slouching around the fleshpots of Gibraltar and before we knew it, those remaining were rattling around like peas in a pod. But this was my big moment and as a young Sub Lieutenant I was left alone on the Bridge to help guide us home. And so, in May 1944, back in Liverpool where I had started, I finally bade farewell to this gracious Lady. For the first two and a half years of my apprenticeship life, I had been taught and trained by my fellow men; had spent nearly all of the 880 nights onboard; had

HMS Warspite. Photograph courtesy of the Imperial War Museum, London. FL22112.

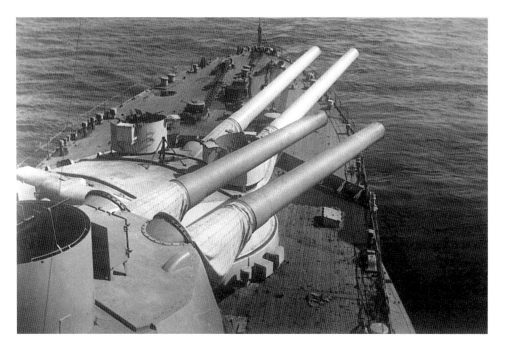

HMS Warspite. Photograph courtesy of the Imperial War Museum, London. FL22134.

travelled thousands of miles away from those who I loved; had learnt how to dine with a Governor and to sup soup standing up in a raging gale; had censored letters of men twice my age and who I knew well; had learnt fear, excitement, boredom and homesickness. WARSPITE had been my Mother and Father.

WEST AFRICA

At this stage in the war, time could not be afforded for the customary long specialist courses and, after a few weeks leave, I duly reported to the Navigation school HMS DRYAD to undergo a shortened navigation course which would, hopefully, provide me with sufficient knowledge to lead an escort squadron of destroyers and frigates. The leader of the 56th Escort squadron, HMS ABERDEEN, was in Bermuda refitting. And so, back to the USA, this time in the magnificent liner, now troopship, QUEEN ELIZABETH. 16000 personnel, two allocated daily meal times (0700 and 1500!!), was hardly my idea of a cruise but at least we got there. After three exciting days in New York, a small new American minesweeper was to be my home for the journey to Bermuda. But hurricanes and very small tin cans do not really mix, and my trunk with all my worldly possessions was swept from the open deck and claimed by Davy Jones.

Bermuda must be one of the most beautiful places on this earth and three exotic weeks passed by in a flash. Too good to last and then back over the Atlantic to join the remainder of the squadron in one of the most dismal, hot and uninteresting places to be found, namely Freetown, Sierra Leone, West Africa. This was to be our base for interminable months, providing little relief from our assigned task of protection of dangerous Atlantic convoys. Best summed up as short periods of action and then boredom. The sinking of a submarine and then being nearly sunk by the new German acoustic torpedo; four spells in hospital with malaria; the absence of sugar for four months and a further encounter with the French.

The small Free French submarine, LA VESTAILLE, had been one of those who chose to join the allies and was directed to work with our forces operating in the area. She required a liaison officer. Having had a dubious school certificate pass in French, my lords and masters considered I was an ideal person for this task. Four French officers and four bunks – where was I to sleep? Gaulloise Bleu cigarettes everywhere; food dripping with oil and red wine flowing; a pig in the forward torpedo space being fattened up for Christmas. All good training, I was informed, after my six months spell was completed. I had had the experience of flying over the sea and now sailing under it. I still preferred to travel on it.

As has already been explained, my intention, on leaving my school, Pangbourne Nautical College, was to become a career naval officer, but the war put paid to that initially, and I was commissioned as a Reserve Officer. To my great excitement, shortly before leaving West Africa, I was informed that I was one of six applicants amongst many, who had now been transferred to the regular Navy. And so, everything comes to an end and, after what seemed a great deal longer than 18 months in these unsavoury waters, I was finally sent home to complete my Sub Lieutenants courses as a regular career Naval Officer. During this period I met, and married, Susan, a young Wren Officer.

GREENOCK

My first appointment as a fully fledged Lieutenant with worldwide experience and solid training, was one which brought considerable excitement – that of standing by one of the new Battle Class Destroyers, HMS GRAVELINES being built at Cammel Laird shipyard in Greenock. An interesting and challenging first few months of marriage, living in a B&B with a powerfully smelling tannery on one side and a distressing slaughterhouse on the other. But it was an instructive period witnessing the dockyard skills in putting together a powerful man of war and finally the day came when we were to set off, with me as navigator, on our sea trials before acceptance. But it was not to be our day and within a few hours there was a loud crack and the brand new astern turbine had split asunder. Back to the drawing board.

ROTHESAY

Young Officers were too valuable to be left with time on their hands and so, back to sea, this time as navigator of another destroyer HMS ONSLAUGHT. She was to be based at Rothesay in the Isles of Bute and I was able to be accompanied by my wife and young son, Richard. But to a young girl living in strange and, very often, bleak surroundings, a husband who only appeared momentarily and temporarily, it was not considered the greatest luxury.

The main submarine training base had been established at Rothesay. Activities there and in surrounding waters, included trial deep dives of new submarines, anti submarine war exercises and formation of new tactics. For most of these, a surface target/escort was required and this was to be our task. During these two years I learned to fear and respect the awesome might of the North Atlantic waters.

Every six months or so, naval officers arrived for the well named Perishers Course, established to determine the fitness or otherwise of rising Officers to take command of a submarine. This intensive course, led by a Senior Officer, involved tactics, days on the Attack Teacher and practical days in submarines with high speed vessels as targets. And so it was that one day we found ourselves twisting and turning at high speed presenting a target to these fairly young gentleman at the end of their course.

It was the day of live firings. Torpedoes are expensive weapons and with the destructive charge removed from the nose and replaced with compressed air of 3000lbs per square foot, the torpedo at the end of its run, can rise to the surface to be collected and returned for another firing the next day. But this charge, as will be explained, is also pretty powerful. The torpedo is set to run below the target destroyer but, so as to ensure this, firing by the student must not be made under 200 yards. Sadly, on this specific day, enthusiasm overcame caution and the 200 yards was reduced.

On such days as this the Navigator spends most of his time on the bridge. But all must eat and, eventually, I disappeared to the wardroom for sustenance. The wardroom in the O type destroyers was situated aft just in front of the rudder and propellors. As my soup was placed before me there was a loud crash, a rumbling and drastic reduction of speed. Climbing to the bridge in haste I was informed that a torpedo had hit a propeller, entered the hull and was sticking out of our side like a pimple. When a torpedo leaves the tube, the engine is started by means of a ratchet being released. It transpired later, that the first torpedo fired had failed to start the engine, the second rammed it, turned it on its side and instead of running sweetly beneath our keel, had set its sights firmly on us like a determined shark. After counterflooding it became clear we were not in danger of sinking but the Base Commander was reported to have needed oxygen when he received our 'naughty' wartime signal of AM TORPEDOED STARBOARD SIDE AFT! Altogether an expensive peacetime accident but, I am confident, pretty unique to be torpedoed in peace time by our own side. Friendly fire, engineering malfunction or misguided perisher? Who knows but it still makes me smile!

GREECE

Back to sea again, this time as second in command (and later in command) of HMS SYLVIA, an ocean going minesweeper. The Germans had laid a large number of mines outside virtually all entrances to the Grecian ports and clearly these had to be removed. A large squadron of eight minesweepers and three danlayers had been formed in Malta specifically for this task. Once again an accompanied posting but with three monthly periods away and considerably less time at base, still not a settled home.

Mines at sea are either moored to set at an appropriate height below the surface; or are magnetic to be exploded by a ship's magnetic field; or are acoustic to be set off by the noises made by a ship's propeller. For the first, the danlayers lay markers well inside the 'safe water'. Fortunately we had access to the detailed charts of these fields. The leading minesweeper begins by steaming well outside the minefield, towing its 'sweep' which is propelled sideways by a contraption known as an otter. The remaining vessels follow in behind this sweep until, as the last is reached, a sizeable area is being swept. Finally, when the other edge of the field has been reached, the eight ships proceed line abreast through the field, tied together with sweep wires from one ship to the next. This final check allows for the field to be declared empty. I never did find out what would happen when a mine had escaped the previous sweep wires! For magnetic mines large electric cables are towed astern to neutralise the magnetic fields, and for dealing with the acoustics, chattering metal pipes are towed astern to produce a greater noise than that produced by the propellors.

In two years of three monthly sessions, over 2000 moored, magnetic and acoustic mines were destroyed with little damage to the squadron. Dodgy yes, but the danger money was nice!

Two major personal events occurred during this period, one each at the end of the spectrum. Firstly Richard, our first born, was killed by a terrible accident in the hotel where my wife and her son were living, and, secondly, Iona our daughter, was born. Sadly I was at sea at both of these of times and they brought home a stark reality of the separation to be suffered when serving at sea in the Royal Navy. The carriage home by RAF Lancaster aircraft and travel from landing to the funeral with the small coffin at my feet, was a day of horror. The arrival of little over 4lbs, Iona, was a joy and helped greatly to moderate my grief.

SCANDINAVIA. EUROPE. MEDITERRANEAN

And so back to the UK to find that, clearly, life ashore was not meant for me and, with only a few weeks to catch my breath, I was on my way to Ireland to join up with the heavy cruiser HMS DEVONSHIRE. By the time cadets leave the training college at Dartmouth, they are well educated but require practical experience before joining the fleet. Accordingly they spend two terms at sea in the training cruiser, currently at that time, HMS DEVONSHIRE. Split into four divisions of some 30 cadets, they complete a a rigorous six months experiencing every aspect of shipboard life which, they, and those under them, will come across in their future. Each of these divisions has a Lieutenant Commander and a Lieutenant (me) to nurse, harass and instill knowledge. As it was only nine years since I had been one of those cadets it was a proud moment and also, at times, a humbling one. One of the big advantages of this important appointment, was that the year was divided into three, with a 'cruise' spent in the Mediterranean in the Autumn, Scandinavia and Northern Europe in the summer and The Caribbean in the spring. Join the Navy and see the world.

PORTSMOUTH

For the first seven years of my married life, I spent no more than a few weeks of each year, with my wife and family. They were living in disagreeable B&B accommodation or small rented houses in parts of England or areas of the world strange to them. A situation of separation which undoubtedly contributed to the sadder tale which is to follow.

At last it had become noticed that I was growing webbed feet and the following two years were to be spent lecturing and instructing – again another change of course and which I began in fear and trepidation.

Disciplinary matters change with behaviour within the country as a whole. Administration needs constant updating and personnel matters are important to all. And so a steady stream of Officers, including those just about to take

OFFICERS DIVISIONAL COURSE.
STAFF. DECEMBER 1953.

| L.T. B.M. TOBEY. R.N. | | SNR. CMD. GNR (G) V. CRUSE. R.N. |
| LT. CDR. A.A. PEARSE. R.N. | LT. CDR. J.D. CARTWRIGHT. R.N. | LT. P.P.P. NEALE. R.N. |

Staff, Officers Divisional Course.

command, were sent to us on The Officers Divisional Course, for a rigorous two week course. Never before had I faced a class of expectant gentleman, many considerably more experienced than I, and it was a little time before I mounted the platform with equanimity. How thankful I was going to be later, when regular after dinner speeches were to be expected every month for two years.

At last my family and I were able to lead what might be called a normal existence and our third child, Andrew, enriched our lives.

GREENWICH

Suddenly I received news for which I had been hoping – an appointment to undergo staff training at The Royal Naval Staff College at Greenwich. The tenor was set immediately by an arrival at 5pm on a Sunday followed by attendance in a classroom after supper and being ordered to precis a long report. Such pressure was to continue the nine long months, and bedtime was invariably never before 3a.m. From strutting and self important gold braided gentlemen, we were back at school again.

Greenwich college is, of course, one of the showpiece buildings in the country. From the painted hall to the chapel to the Thames waterfront, it is a place of magnificence and we felt very privileged to be part of it, in my case, for the second time. The entire walls and ceiling of the Painted Hall (where we were to eat), were painted by a Mr James Thorburn. Having agreed to a fixed price contract, after many years, he realised that he had not received a sufficient return for his art and applied to the Admiralty for an increase. Being curtly refused he calmly painted himself in at the bottom corner of the end wall, holding out his hand!

The eventual award of the qualification "Passed Staff College (PSC)" after one's name in the Navy List, was noted with pride.

PORTSMOUTH

The North Atlantic Treaty Organisation (NATO) was, by now, a rapidly growing, and important, Alliance, and I was now about to be indoctrinated into its workings. Commander-in-Chief Channel's headquarters were situated in HM Dockyard Portsmouth and staffed by British, French, Belgian and Dutch personnel. Whilst doctrine had to be written, what was laid down had to be practised and paper and live exercises were carried out regularly. As Staff Officer Plans (Training) my task was to formulate these exercises. An interesting appointment which was to hold me in good stead in the future.

MEDITERRANEAN

Equally good news was to follow (back to sea of course) when directions came to join HMS DEFENDER as second in command. Eight of these large new destroyers were being built. They were the pride of the fleet all commanded by Captains and the appointment as the second in command was quite likely to lead to promotion and a brass hat.

I have hinted above that our marriage was sometimes bumping on rocks below the surface. The endless separation with wife and two young children living in sub standard accommodation; the return of the warrior from time to time, probably never fully appreciating the situation, were both to lead to suspicions, doubt and boredom. Whilst I was overjoyed at looking forward to my next two years, it soon became apparent that my wife and I were drawing apart. By the time I was to arrive back in the UK, the marriage was over.

By now the Mediterranean had become my second home and the time spent in DEFENDER was both interesting and constructive.

In the early 1950s, the Priest Makarios became Archbishop of Cyprus and, de facto, leader of the Greek Cypriot community. He was soon to become the leading advocate of union with Greece and, ultimately, Independence. The British Government were reluctant to de-colonise the island which had become their new headquarters for the Middle East. It was not long before a new resistance movement, EOKA was formed which, in turn, required a good supply of arms in order to carry out its operation against the British forces. To prevent supply by sea of these weapons, the Cyprus patrol was established of which DEFENDER played her part. One could not help feeling sorry for the small fishing boats being stopped and searched in the middle of the night by a large and menacing warship. But it had to be done and certainly was a success.

At last came the news that most, (but not I think, me) were waiting for, namely that we were to return to the UK. By this time the virulent Asian flu was sweeping Europe and sure enough, as we arrived in Gibraltar for a brief fuelling stop, several of our ship's company were hit by the dreaded lurgy. One of the moles (breakwaters) at Gibraltar is detached and this is where we lay for an interminable age, not being allowed ashore. Eventually 98% of the ship's company succumbed, including yours truly.

Eventually we were to arrive back in Chatham with, for me, the most conflicting of emotions. Firstly that my next task was to disentangle the marriage and secondly to celebrate my promotion to Commander. At this point I must express my grateful thanks to my Mother and Father who helped me in every way possible, to re-establish myself.

Some explanation is required here concerning the method of promotion in The Royal Navy. Barring accidents and stupidity, promotion up to Lieutenant Commander is automatic and by time. Thereafter it is by selection. Twice a year after three years in that rank, promotion to Commander is made to a number of Officers. The similar process takes place later for promotions to Captain. Understandably, those who are promoted earlier in the 'zone', are likely to climb higher.

After the war, a large number of warships were scrapped or sold off, but an equally large number of senior officers were left fighting for command of those ships remaining. In turn, this left such officers with, possibly, only one command. With rapidly advancing technologies and continuous review of tactics, a larger number of groundings and collisions, were occurring. It was decided therefore to nominate certain officers upon promotion to be WET and others as DRY. Those on the wet list could expect to receive more than one sea command as a Commander and Captain, whilst those on the Dry list would probably spend the rest of their time in the service commanding shore establishments or in staff appointments. As the raison d'etre for joining the navy was basically for going to sea, this could be a considerable disappointment. The earlier the promotion, the more likely it was that further promotion would follow and thus most of those to be promoted on the wet list, headed the list of names. Likewise further promotion to those on the Dry list was going to become more unlikely. However, in order to prevent complete disillusionment, a few of the brighter officers found themselves near the top of the list but on the Dry list. In my case, with promotion coming fairly early, but being placed on the Dry list, my euphoria quickly evaporated with the realisation that it was unlikely that I was to go to sea ever again and that further promotion would not be so easy. There were many others like me and, eventually and after some years, a high powered team was given the task of producing a suitable answer. This they did, and today the system is altered very little from what had been perfectly acceptable for many years before. An option here was to retire early but with two small children still to be educated and imponderables as to obtaining a job, I decided to serve further.

LONDON

Having 'lost' Singapore in 1942, it was appreciated that the situation in The Far East was far from being stable. Equally it was evident that little thought had been given to the ability, or otherwise, of the United Kingdom forces to provide assistance in the event of further conflict. Accordingly a small joint service staff was formed, headed by an Air Vice Marshal and with me as the Naval representative. This was my first appointment in Whitehall and I was soon to learn of the intrigues, machinations and serious undertakings of the complicated political machine. The study was to last over a year resulting, finally, in a three day presentation at the Royal Air Force Station, Cranwell. This was to be attended by virtually all the Top Brass of the three services. It was proposed by the Air Marshal, that this galaxy of talent should be flown from London to Cranwell in the newly arrived Air Force version of the Comet. In view of past history of this aircraft, it was felt desirable to obtain the agreement of the Chief of Defence Staff, then Admiral Mountbatten. As the naval member I was directed to present our case to the great man and, at one stage, voiced the possibility of severe losses of top personnel in the event of an accident. "Don't know why you should worry Commander," was the retort from the Admiral, "would be good for your promotion"! And so we went ahead.

Whilst working long hours, life with a flat only two underground stops from the office, was a big change from the hurly burly of shipboard life. I suppose it was only inevitable in the big metropolis, that I was to meet someone with whom I felt a great affinity. She, Elizabeth, held the highly paid and responsible job as UK Bureau Chief of the Canadian paper, Montreal Star, Not many months after we met, we were married in London in 1959 and I moved into her spacious flat in Sloane Square.

MALTA

Life is never entirely simple and before we knew it, my task in Whitehall came to an end and a telephone call provided us with the news that I was to be posted back to Malta, but this time ashore. My wife was now pregnant and although a great deal of soul searching was required, the joint decision was taken that she would resign from her London job and devote the remainder of her life to that of a sailor's consort. The considerable loss of salary and thus a lowering of our standard of life also had to be overcome!

In October 1959, my career took another turning. Whilst I had experience of life at sea, and had been assigned other tasks ashore, they had all had connections with the Royal Navy. This time I was drafted to The Headquarters, Allied Forces Mediterranean (HAFMED). My brief was to run the Public relations Office.

HAFMED had been established some time earlier. Malta was then a self governing colony. Foreign Affairs and Defence were reserved to her Majesty's Government. Welcomed by, and with the full approval of, the then government of Malta, HAFMED drew the hostility of the Malta Labour Party, led by Dom Mintoff.

Mr Mintoff was a political gladiator to his fingertips. He made repeated sallies in the area of foreign policy, initially by well publicized contacts with Colonel Nasser in Egypt and Colonel Gaddafi in Libya. Subsequently, he made overtures to Mao's China, and the less reputable East European Communist leaders like Ceausescu of Romania. Mintoff played his political poker game with aplomb, alternately in the name of "independence", "neutrality" and "national interest".

Mintoff's bullish politics polarized the island. The pro-western elements drew towards each other on the principle that when bad men unite, the good must associate.

HQ Allied Forces Mediterranean.

The most outspoken supporter of Malta's British connections and pro-West advocate, was the redoubtable Mabel Strickland (part English, part Maltese and daughter of Lord Strickland, one-time Prime minister of Malta). She also controlled The Times of Malta.

Mintoff became Prime Minister in 1955, only to resign in 1959, having collided with the British Government over the issue of UK Department redundancies. He was hailed as the leader of the Malta Liberation Movement.

There being no political party willing and able to form a majority in the Malta Parliament, The Malta Constitution was suspended, much to the consternation of genuine democratic opinion in the island.

The stage was thus set for a battle of wills. It was at this point that I found myself in the eye of the vortex as I took over the job of Chief of Public Information at HAFMED in October 1959. My staff comprised one American naval officer, one Italian civilian, one Greek librarian, one American photographer and an English Wren as secretary.

Our mission was to project the best image of NATO and what it stood for, and to see that the image was not sullied, maliciously or otherwise. Our brief was to keep strictly out of partisan politics. At the same time, I took the view that we should not stay aloof in the face of misrepresentation, deliberate or otherwise, by politicians, or insinuations by media hacks.

The accent of our activities was on positive information initiatives. Lectures, film shows, essay competitions amongst all the schools in the island, and articles in The Times of Malta soon began to have their effect, and there were not many days where the print media would be devoid of verbal fisticuffs between me and NATO's detractors.

Our most outspoken champion was Mabel Strickland herself – a formidable force who learned all she knew from her tenacious father, and whose political career during the 20's and 30's was as stormy as that of Dom Mintoff in the 60's and 70's. Together with a sense of purpose and true grit, she had a sense of fun. I recall various occasions at her Palazzo in Lija when, after lunch, the guests were shown her party trick of hypnotizing one of the chickens!

Mabel was a useful and valued ally. But our overriding objective was to withstand and counteract the remorseless psychological war then being waged against NATO and against Western values. It was necessary to draw Maltese public opinion into the argument we were raising.

Malta, not yet having full independent status, there was no possibility of forming a Maltese branch of the Atlantic Alliance. But there was no reason why a branch of the British Atlantic Committee (a UK publicity forum for the Alliance), should not have its own offspring in Malta. So, after a few months, this was formally constituted, with an elected Chairman and Committee – an inaugural membership of some 200.

I would like to think that this core initiative played some part in activating and consolidating the forces which cherished democratic sentiments that, eventually, flowered in the movement for Malta's EC accession.

I was pleased to receive the personal thanks from The Secretary General of the North Atlantic Treaty Association in Paris and from the Supreme Allied Commander in Europe, General Norstaad.

Further gratification was to come when visiting Malta with my wife, 46 years later. I presumed that The Times of Malta, main paper of the island and my mouthpiece against Mintoff, would have information concerning any of the Malta Branch of The British Atlantic Committee I had established those years ago. I wrote to the Editor to enquire whether any of the personnel involved were still active, and told him where we would be staying and that I would contact him after my arrival. To my astonishment, upon buying the paper at the airport, I found that my letter had been published in its entirety on that

From: Brigadier E.B.W. Cardiff, C.B.E.

SUPREME HEADQUARTERS ALLIED POWERS EUROPE
GRAND QUARTIER GÉNÉRAL DES PUISSANCES ALLIÉES EN EUROPE
PARIS. FRANCE

19th April, 1960.

My Dear Tony

    Thank you very much for the cuttings you sent me on the Paris visit.

    I must congratulate you on your enterprise and the success of the trip. I think the reports, generally speaking, were excellent and there can be no doubt that the visit did an immense amount of good. General Norstad told me that he was tremendously impressed by the very complimentary remarks he heard on all sides about your efforts.
He was also interested to meet the man who has qualified for the NATO fellowship.

    I can well imagine your feeling of looking forward to a let up. However, you have started something so big that I think you will find it difficult to put the break on.

    Again, my very grateful thanks to you for all you have done and also for keeping me so well informed of the results of the visit.

Yours Sin

Ernő Cardiff

Commander A.A. Pearse, R.N.
Chief of Public Information Division,
Allied Forces Mediterranean,
Malta.

Gratefully received.

very day. The telephone never stopped ringing and although our holiday was marred somewhat, it was a delight to renew acquaintance with so many. With Mr Mintoff still alive, I wondered whether there would be any comment from his direction. He never raised his head above the parapet.

Whilst still at the NATO headquarters (now 1960), my new wife presented me with a son, William, the second of my children to be born in the Military Hospital, Mtarfa in Malta. It was a joy that, on this occasion, I had my feet firmly on dry land and was able to engage fully with all the activities of a new family.

CORSHAM

As already explained I had little expectation of returning to sea but one morning shortly after I had arrived in my office just after I had completed two years with NATO, I had a telephone call from The Admiralty to say that I was to be appointed in command of one of the only two independent shore commands open to an Officer of Commander rank. This was to be The Petty Officers Leadership School in Corsham, Wiltshire.

A young naval rating advances from Able Seaman rate to Leading Seaman and, hopefully, to Petty Officer. At this stage he will be directly responsible for the leading, administration and wellbeing of a considerable number of juniors. Whether he be of a technical branch, operations or cook, he is unlikely to have had any experience in such leadership matters.

Every six weeks 24 Petty Officers would be sent to me from all over the Fleet and would then spend anything up to 18 hours a day in classroom techniques including the art of teaching; the writing of letters and synopsis; sport; welfare matters and, finally, a gruelling five days in the Black Mountains in Wales under the most rigorous of conditions. It was gratifying indeed to watch the steady growth in physical and mental stature of these young men and the majority unquestionably returned to the Fleet considerably better equipped to carry out their duties. It would be nice if all young men today could be given such an opportunity. I used to be asked whether I thought leadership could be taught in six weeks. For some probably not, but after being at ROYAL ARTHUR, they could not complain that they had not been told what was expected of them!

With some months in comfort in London, two years pleasure in the lovely Malta and now, a further two years in glorious Wiltshire with a pleasant house and cook and steward (the required entertaining was considerable), my wife was beginning to feel that she had made the right decision in giving up her

HMS Royal Arthur.

HMS Royal Arthur.

rewarding and responsible career. But there is always something somewhere which will give you a kick in the teeth and this arrived with the news that a Staff Officer Administration on the staff of Flag Officer Middle East, was required sooner rather than later, in Aden!

ADEN

As was happening all round the globe, the desire for Independence was gathering speed and Yemen could see no reason why the British should continue to rule their country and so began a steady and mounting onslaught against our Forces in the area. To combat this, the number of troops, ships and aircraft increased tenfold bringing with them enormous problems of administration. These were accentuated by the fact that Aden is a hot, unwelcoming environment with little to excite or maintain morale of the soldiery. Perhaps the song of Tom Jones may be remembered with the line of 'The Barren Rocks of Aden'.

Up to now in my naval career, I had been more than satisfied with the positions in which I found myself. But the problem of the lack of suitable

Aden.

accommodation, the erection of shark nets so that swimming could be safe, the explosion of grenades being thrown at cars and the transport of one's children to school in buses covered in wire netting with an armed guard on the door, all produced an air of melancholy and sadness. Two particular incidents affected us considerably. Firstly the Senior Royal Air Force medical officer was killed by a grenade thrown through his house window during a party for one of his children. And then, a very large explosion occurred outside the Officers mess. An electrical transmitting station had been blown up. I don't know why we worry about our children – our 5 year old, playing outside with another child, in answer reaction to a frantic query as to his well being was "Oh Mum, it was only a bomb"!

The story can now be told of a Petty Officer's wife, a nurse, and whose husband was away at sea, who had been working in a medical centre in the native quarter of Crater on the outskirts of Aden. One morning two young men were carried in with bullet wounds and other injuries. It became clear that these had been engaged by British forces and were two "terrorists". They had not known that one of the nurses treating them was the wife of a British serviceman and that she had an interpreter with her. During her care she learnt a considerable amount about further operations being planned against the British. With commendable bravery she reported this to the authorities who realised immediately that she could be in danger, especially living alone as she was. I was directed to go to her house at 0600 in the morning and take her into custody before she was to board an aircraft to the UK later in the day. She was to leave in 15 minutes, take only a small grip and if she objected I was to show her my pistol. No time to contact her husband, she must leave all her possessions and leave the house with little more than the nightie she was wearing. I heard later that she was amply rewarded but the shock to her and her husband must have been considerable. For me, it was one of the most unpleasant episodes of my life.

The one redeeming feature of life in Aden was an annual free 14 day trip down to Kenya for the whole family. And it was during this period that one of the strange co-incidences in life which seem to beset us all, began to unravel.

At this time, independence for Kenya was taking place, and HM Government was announcing what measures would be taken to assist the Kenyans in this transition. One of these was the building up or even, in the case of the sea and air, forming, armed forces, and the loan of training teams to bring such forces up to a required standard. The Kenyan Army had been in existence for many years and the Army Commander was a Kenyan General. Likewise

BATKEN, the British Army training team was well established with a Major General at its head. He, in turn, was to become Chief of General Staff of all three forces.

In Mombasa, the large port in the south of the country, the Royal Navy owned a large and sophisticated ammunition and supply depot which had been used to supply British forces in the area. It was decided to donate this real estate to the Kenyans but it was felt that some of the equipment would not be needed by them or could be better used by ourselves. The Kenyan theatre was administered by Middle East Headquarters and, being responsible for administration, who better than Staff Officer Admin to carry out this exercise? And so I found myself travelling to Mombasa to compile lists of what equipment I thought we should remove before handover.

Amongst a considerable number of items, I directed that one of the large harbour launches should be transported to Aden where such was urgently required. A similar need was for a proper refrigerator for our house in Aden and so the smart piece of machinery I found in the house of the Director of the depot, similarly found its way there. The rest of the story I shall leave until later.

During our two year stay, HM Forces in Aden had been increased to a very large number but in spite of this, operations up country in the Radfan area continued and life in Aden itself became unpleasant. But most things come to an end and, nationally the time came eventually for HM Government to withdraw and, personally for us to return to UK.

PLYMOUTH

HMS DRAKE is a large naval barracks in Plymouth and after our leave, we found ourselves in a pleasant married quarter and with me as No 2 of this establishment. Like all military complexes it was a complicated mixture of service life. Personnel standing by ships refitting; the Hydrographic School; the Physical Training School; Court Martial Rooms; Pay Offices; The Royal Marine Band; The Plymouth Field Gun Crew. All with their aims and wishes and self pride and all requiring welding into the bigger picture. The Wardroom, home of many Officers, contained one of the most beautiful dining rooms to be found anywhere and where the Commander (me) reigned supreme. Earlier I pointed out that later in my career I would be confronted with the need for regular after dinner speaking. These dinners were to occur monthly and although there were guests to be referred to, another 50 or more Officers were present who had also been there for one, two or many more months

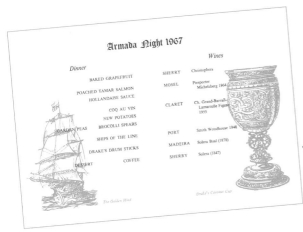

Armada Night 1967

Dinner	Wines

BAKED GRAPEFRUIT

POACHED TAMAR SALMON
HOLLANDAISE SAUCE

COQ AU VIN
NEW POTATOES
BROCOLLI SPEARS
GARDEN PEAS

SHIPS OF THE LINE

DRAKE'S DRUM STICKS

DESSERT COFFEE

SHERRY Christophers

MOSEL Piesporter Michelsberg 1964

CLARET Ch. Grand-Barrall-Lamarzelle Figeac 1955

PORT Smith Woodhouse 1948

MADEIRA Solera Bual (1878)

SHERRY Solera (1847)

The Golden Hind

Drake's Coconut Cup

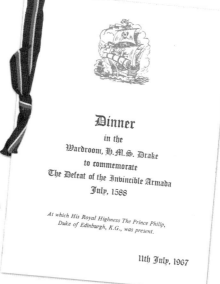

Dinner
in the
Wardroom, H.M.S. Drake
to commemorate
The Defeat of the Invincible Armada
July, 1588

*At which His Royal Highness The Prince Philip,
Duke of Edinburgh, K.G., was present.*

11th July, 1967

Drake Armada dinner.

Plymouth Field Gun Crew.

previously. Repetition had to be avoided and fresh jokes found – a challenge. Sir Francis Drake was remembered annually at a dinner and, rising to my feet to introduce The Duke of Edinburgh, a naval officer himself and one with an acerbic reputation, was not a moment of joy.

KENYA

In early 1967, my wife and I received an invitation (a Command actually), to dinner at Admiralty House. Whilst not necessarily unusual, it is sensible to find out whether this was to be pleasure or business and I was then informed that The Kenyan Minister of Defence, Dr Mungai, would be present and that my wife and I were to be introduced.

Earlier I stated that HM Government had agreed to provide a Training Team to help establish a Kenyan navy in Mombasa. Commander Max Walker had been appointed to lead a Royal Naval party of some 25 Officers and 50 Chief and Petty Officers. Training had taken place firstly in UK with some Kenyan Officers being sent to Dartmouth, but eventually the whole team plus families were moved to Mombasa. The normal maximum time to be spent on any one appointment is two and a half to three years and Commander Walker required a relief. And evidently it was thought my face would fit. Two months later this appointment was approved by The Kenya Government and in September 1966 my wife, one son and self were on our way to Mombasa.

And so, once again, I was to direct my poor old brain in another direction. In addition to their Training role, all the UK personnel were to carry operational duties until there were suitably trained Kenyans to take over from them. All the four large patrol craft, given to Kenya by HM Government (three more paid for by Kenya to be added later), were commanded by British Officers. Similarly my title was to be that of Commander Kenya Navy and Commanding Officer RN Training team. Clearly, for the former, especially as I was to wear Kenya uniform, I would owe allegiance to The Kenyan President and with the latter, my boss was still the Queen. Whilst my normal pay was the responsibility of Her Majesty, my expenses were paid by Kenya. And if (and I had many such visits), a UK task force arrived in Mombasa then the poor Admiral had to pay customary respects in full sword and medal dress, to me!

Mombasa with President Kenyatta.

Such an arrangement could produce anomalies and, sometimes, difficulties. Clearly what emerged would be a Navy brought up the British way but incorporating Kenyan customs and wishes. In the event, there was only one

Jamhuri (Freedom Day). Author being introduced to the Crowd.

serious and diplomatic incident which I shall relate in due course. The real joy in all this was one which every male relishes – responsibility.

No Admiralty to consult and, as a 'foreigner' I was only allowed in the office of the sole RN representative in Mombasa, by invitation. But I suppose my biggest enjoyment came, in metaphorically cocking a snook at The Wet and Dry lists. Whilst a large part of my time was spent in political and administrative matters, I had ships in which to go to sea and, in the time that I was there we carried out flag showing visits to Seychelles, Madagascar, Mauritius and The Comores.

But, in addition to the heavy training tasks, the Navy was operationally busy. As stated already, Tanzania and Kenya did not see eye to eye and one of the ships was on permanent station down near the Tanzanian border. Smuggling and piracy was rife in the north off Somalia and another vessel was on constant standby in Lamu.

The more earnest of the readers will have noted my references to The Admiralty Ammunition and Stores Depot in Mombasa and to my sending back to Aden a year or two ago, a large harbour launch and a refrigerator. My family was now installed in the old Director's house which had housed the

President Haile Selassie of Ethiopia.

20th Anniversary of the Navy.

fridge and which my wife now wanted. And, as our house and the base were on the mainland, as many boats as possible were required to take us all back and forth to Mombasa which is an island. Never forget – whilst you may be unaware, someone, somewhere, will be following your every move and events will come back to haunt you!

People often ask me my opinions of President Kenyatta, especially in view of his previous activities with Mau Mau. Cleverly sidestepping the latter problem, I always reply with my genuine admiration for the man. During my monthly audience and when, sometimes, I was able to proudly proclaim that we were now in a position to dispense with one more of the British personnel, I was reminded that his people needed more training than some might understand, and that I was not to go so fast. Although he and his wife were undoubtedly a rich couple, corruption in general was never allowed to flourish and Kenya only started to emulate most other African countries, once he had died.

Three further points would indicate his pragmatic qualities. Installed in State House, Nairobi, was a Colonial policeman who, in the past, had been his jailor during imprisonment by the British. Probably a slight exaggeration but

Kenya defence hierarchy.

it was rumoured that his trusted friend was the last to wish him goodnight and the first to pronounce a new day.

The President travelled from Mombasa to Nairobi by car (a six hour journey). To welcome him at the gates to the city, the Kenya Navy provided a guard of honour and on completion I was invited to State House, Mombasa to an informal chat with himself and his Ministers.

On another occasion, the whole family, plus my Mother, on a visit from England, were preparing for an afternoon on the beach. As we loaded the car, a call was received which required me to report to The President. As we arrived at the gates, my Minister of Defence stated that we should all follow him into the house. There then followed a one and a half hours talk with the great man explaining to my Mother, the trials and tribulations of being the leader of a nation of so many disparate views.

To those who may have suffered under his leadership in earlier times, these observations may not be understood but they are related as fact.

I referred, above, to the one occasion when I realised that I may be on a collision course with the Administration and actually suggested that my wife

Presidents of Kenya, Zambia, Tanzania.

had better start to pack. When resident at his State coast house at Bamburi, Mombasa, the President required one of his vessels to patrol up and down and around the harbour and State house. Because of the monsoon this could be a hazardous mission and on one occasion I was asked by the Duty Commanding Officer to be allowed to return to harbour. Whatever the President may have required, the security of one of his ships and sailors must be paramount, and I ordered the patrol to be ceased. At midnight I was disturbed by the telephone with the Defence Minister making it perfectly clear to me that the President was highly displeased with my actions. Furthermore I was to present myself at State House the following morning.

Like many of such situations, the reason for the furore was relatively simple in that the Comptroller of The Household had had a merry evening, had noticed the lack of the patrol, and had told His Excellency that his Naval Commander had disobeyed his instructions. A few minutes of explanation and the gloom disappeared. Whilst the Comptroller's future must be considered uncertain, my star rose to the heavens and from that day, any request or answer that I might give to difficult questions, was complied with or accepted without question!

Thorn amongst the roses. Government wives at State House, Nairobi.

Throughout the world, formal visits by ships from one country to another, provide the means for intimate contact and formation of trust. Whilst such visits often are arranged for unusual relaxation for the ships companies, at other times they are prepared with positive ideas in mind.

Whilst the British reigned supreme in Kenya the Soviet navy could only look on, with envy, at the facilities which Mombasa provided. It was hardly surprising therefore, that I was summoned to Nairobi to be informed that a request had been received for a missile cruiser squadron to make a formal visit. My views were requested. I explained that such visits were not unusual and, unless there was any good reason to deny such a visit, then it should be agreed. At that, the President stated that the Russian sailors should not be allowed ashore and, once again, I had to explain that such action would not be understood. I suspected that the Russians themselves would control shore parties severely and in this I was proved right.

The day thus arrived when this impressive array of vessels arrived and an interesting five days were to follow. Understandably I also "wore" my British hat and, as such close contact with such vessels was not often possible in those

Inspection of Soviet guard of honour.

days, my report was of considerable interest to the intelligence forces back home. Had the Russians been able to see it, they would not have been best pleased.

The dramas started as the vessels approached their moorings and considerable difficulties were encountered in getting firmly secured. In full ceremonial dress complete with sword and medals, I, accompanied by the Kenyan Provincial Commissioner, mounted the gangway, inspected the guard of honour and were led below to book signing, speeches and unlimited vodka. It was here that the second mistake was made. The Kenyan PC asked to be shown a missile to which the answer was a firm NIET. Unnecessary as a missile itself is a streamlined lump of metal. A request to see the computer space from where this missile would be despatched, would have been another matter and would have merited a strong denial. On the way back to base in my boat, this rudeness had clearly not been understood.

The Russian Admiral, prior, to the visit, had stated that he wished to hold a lunch at which he hoped all the Government Ministers. Ambassadors and other dignitaries, would, accompanied by their wives, travel down from

Vodka....

And more vodka.

Nairobi to attend. The lunch was to be held on the quarterdeck of one of the large missile vessels alongside which, was moored a destroyer. Whether it is customary in the Russian Navy to test their weapons when being relieved on sentry duty, I know not. But the fact that a high powered lunch was being held on the ship next to it, was of little interest to the duty sentry on the destroyer who let off a few rounds, and shock and horror was in the air.

My wife and I gave a formal dinner party to The Ambassador, The Admiral, four or five Officers and a few other guests. It was on the day that Yuri Gagarin, the first Russian astronaut, was killed in an air crash. I said a few words, the drink flowed, the atmosphere became maudlin and then hilarious. After dinner, my wife was on the sofa being clutched in both arms by the Admiral who was whispering in her ear words which sounded something like "Yellow Blue Vords". The interpreter hastened to tell me that, in Russian, words which sound the same, mean, quite simply, "I love you". To this day I am never quite sure whether my wife was embarrassed or flattered.

An exhausting and anxious five days passed, luckily without any serious incidents and as the ships cast off and set sail, a large Russian built car drove up to our house and my wife was presented with a delightful book of Russian antiquities, containing the inscription:

> "My wife and I will always remember
> the delightful time we spent in your
> house in Mombasa during the
> friendly visit of the warships of the
> USSR to Kenya.
>
> With cordial regards and many thanks,
>
> Yours sincerely,
>
> D. GORYUNOV
> Ambassador of the USSR in the
> Republic of Kenya"

The reader is probably aware of the fact that public servants are not supposed to accept such gifts without permission. And so, with a heavy heart, this presentation was relayed back to UK. Relief and thanks all round when the all clear was given.

Посольство
Союза Советских
Социалистических Республик
"12" December, 1968

Dear sir,

My wife and I will always remember
the delightful time we spent in you
house in Mombasa during the friendly
visit of the warships of the USSR to
Kenya.

With cordial regards and many
thanks,

Yours sincerely,

D.GORYUNOV
Ambassador of the USSR in the Republic
of Kenya

To: Com. A.A.PEARSE
NAVY COMMANDER
Kenya Navy Headquarters

A nice present!

As will be told shortly, I returned to Kenya to attend celebrations in 2005. All my enquiries indicated that in the 37 years which had passed, there had been no similar request for Soviet warships to pay a courtesy visit to Mombasa.

The days passed but not altogether without anxiety. On a formal flag showing visit to the Comores islands, one of the patrol craft had a breakdown. The remainder were ordered to proceed but thereafter, communications were lost with the stricken vessel. Although I did not enjoy having to do it, I requested surveillance assistance from HM forces and a British Maritime patrol aircraft which happened to be operating in the area, was diverted and soon made contact.

Equally dramatic at the time, was the grounding by one of my ships, just off the Tanzanian coast, resulting in a severely damaged propeller. The commanding officer was still a Royal Navy Officer and so, in accordance with tradition, I asked for a Court Martial to be assembled in Mombasa. This involved a Senior Officer from Singapore being sent as President and a considerable amount of organisation. A sledgehammer to crack a nut perhaps, but certainly one more good training example to the young Kenyans. I am pleased to say that the young officer was given a reprimand which, I heard later, had done him no harm as he had reached the rank of Captain.

Kenya is large, the tribes can be proud and independent and communications are not too good. The Agricultural Society of Kenya (ASK) shows which occur in all the major towns throughout the year, are a vital way of bringing enlightenment to the people. In the case of the Navy, a large part of the population live miles from the sea and have no idea that Kenya was now learning to have a Navy.

The shows, whilst mainly being the equivalent of agricultural shows in Britain, also contain large spectacles by the three services. A difficult task for the Navy up country. However with clever camouflaging of lorries as patrol craft, navigation lights flashing in the darkness and naval wireless messages floating in the air, a surprisingly dramatic impression was given and always received with great ovation.

At one of the last ASK's I was to attend, I was seated next to The President as "my" piece was about to start. To my great surprise, the great man lent across to thank me for what I had done and asked me to stay in his country and not to return to the UK. There were also coded signals that a farm would be found for me. Very flattering and exciting, but I was not due to leave the navy for another few years and with a son shortly due to attend higher schools, I reluctantly had to decline.

Farewell to President Kenyatta.

And so the time approached for me to leave this fascinating country. But not before one last bit of sparkle. The President of Liberia, was paying a State visit, part of which was a visit to Mombasa and which entailed guards of honour, a big lunch and the painting of coal. This was successfully completed but with a call, two days later, for my appearance in Nairobi in three hours time, to receive a decoration. Yet again a furious tourist was to be bumped off his seat in his booked aircraft and before I had time to catch breath, I was standing on the lawn of State House to receive (in company with the other Commanders and Chief of Police) and from The President himself, a beautiful neck Order. I had become a Member Of The Star Of Africa. Manufactured in Paris, this is an Order of some magnificence but loses its lustre when my orders from Buckingham Palace forbids its wearing unless in the presence of The Liberian Head of State. Not very likely and I doubt if it will be given an airing before my time comes.

In 1984, an invitation was received to attend celebrations to commemorate the 20th Anniversary of The Kenya Navy and, to my great pleasure, this was repeated in December 2004 at the 40th Anniversary. For the first occasion, the Royal Navy presented three silver bugles, mounted, which belonged, originally, to HMS Kenya, a Royal Navy cruiser. For the second, a beautiful silver tampion, normally fitted, (but not silver), into the muzzle of the main armament when warships are in harbour, with the inscription PRESENTED BY THE PEOPLE OF KENYA TO HMS KENYA. LAUNCHED ON THE 18TH AUGUST 1939. These two beautiful trophies now lie in the Trophy cupboard in Navy Headquarters, Mombasa.

Having spent two and a half years under President Kenyatta and with these trophies being presented to President Moi and then President Kwibaki, I was beginning to feel thoroughly Kenyanised!

The photographs of the first three Kenyan Navy Commanders (all British), still adorn the wall of the Officers Mess anteroom; the unsolicited and generous invitations to return to the country on two occasions; the unstinted support

Three silver bugles, mounted.

Silver tampion.

20th Anniversary Visit, President Moi.

40th Anniversary Visit, President Kwibaki.

Three wise men.

given to me by President Kenyatta's government; and the warm words and grateful thanks spoken by the next two, leave happy memories. We must have done something right!

FAREHAM

By now, realisation had struck me that I was due to retire in six years time; that we had to buy a house and get on the 'ladder'; and that my final job should be one where I was in contact with the commercial world. The first was achieved by buying a house in Hampshire, the second by the fact that the Officer with the task of appointing his peers, was a friend of mine. And thus my run-down was now assured and to my satisfaction.

The Cold War was now very real, nuclear war was very possible and should this happen, how was the country to be protected? Suddenly bolt holes were required for The Government, Civil Defence was given the highest priority and the closest liaison was needed between the armed forces and the police. All this required considerable planning and for the next three years I was to be found with a wet towel round my head trying to solve insurmountable problems. Dealing with plans carrying the very highest security classification, was both exciting and alarming. Exactly what was going to be the punishment for leaving Top Secret documents on the top of a bus? And working underground in an old anti-Napoleonic fort, added to The James Bond atmosphere. But it was an important and interesting task made even more pleasant by being able to settle in to our first house.

SOUTHAMPTON

In time of war the Naval Control of Shipping organisation is vital to ensuring that supplies to and from the UK can be maintained. Lessons from World War II can never be forgotten and the subordination of commercial maritime interests to naval control, would have to be re-introduced in the event of further conflict.

Whilst London in peacetime, had the Admiralty to provide planning and co-ordination, Liverpool, Cardiff, Glasgow, and Southampton required a naval presence and a Naval Liaison Officer was ensconced in each. In peace he was to liaise and exercise with the commercial shipping, and to represent the Navy. In wartime this officer would become Naval Officer in Charge (of a port) and be responsible for the whole of the naval control of shipping in that area.

As stated already, careful planning had taken place and with The Naval Liaison Officer at Southampton retiring in three years time, I slipped into his shoes with little fuss.

Whilst I was determined to carry out my naval duties to the best of my ability, it was only natural that my thoughts turned also, to the day of my retirement. Naval pensions, whilst secure and non-contributory during service, were minuscule when paid out and 53 years of age is too young to be doing nothing. I had always been interested in travel, and an old friend of mine and also recently retired from the Royal Navy, had, only a year or two before, opened a Travel Agency in Hampshire. Accordingly I signed up to a correspondence course in the subject which filled many of my out of office hours. Actually I was surprised at the depth of the subject and was amused (and dismayed) at some of the red ink splashed across my returned documents (put there by a 20 year old girl or retired professor?) Who did they think they were "talking" to?! I had progressed about half way, when my life, once again, was to be turned upside down.

One of the most famous, and respected clubs, to be found in Southampton, is the Master Mariners Club. Open to all mariners with membership including all the well known Commanders of the mighty liners. As the Naval Liaison officer to the commercial shipping world, I was soon invited to join and spent most of my lunchtimes and many dinners and functions in their company. Annually, a sumptuous lunch, attended by over 200, was held in one of the liners visiting the port. I say was, as I do not know how they manage today with cruise liners being in port for only a matter of hours.

The guest of honour was to be The Commander in Chief, Portsmouth, and a friend of mine. He was now also my boss. Not surprisingly he asked me to draft a suitable speech and, never missing an opportunity, I included a request that he bid my farewells to the port of Southampton, although retirement was not quite yet.

Beginning at midday, the liquid lunch continued until well into the afternoon, at which point I was invited to return to The Master Mariners' Club. By early evening I had been approached by two gentleman with inquisitive minds, and by late evening arrived back home to be met with a not unnaturally enquiring wife. A little more drink than was wise, coupled with an excited but whirling mind, gave me a disturbed night.

Crest Nicholson plc was a large group welding together a range of companies from home building to tennis courts and from long established yacht builders to marinas where the products could be parked. Camper and Nicholsons Marine Equipment Ltd was one of these companies, supplying the yachting and commercial world with equipment ranging from liferafts to charts and lifebuoys to sextants.

Good businesses never stand still and the increase in the number of countries forming their own navies, had been noted. Presumably, a good deal of equipment was required by these shipbuilders worldwide, somewhere along the line. Furthermore a rumour that the current NLO had been involved in one of these navies was also prevalent and perhaps a match could be made in heaven? Thus, nine months before my release from the navy, I was to accept a post as Sales and Marketing Executive, Camper and Nicholsons Marine Equipment Ltd.

After nearly three years in a surprisingly rewarding and interesting job as Naval Liaison officer Southampton, I was to be surprised to be given, by Union Castle Line, a first class voyage to Las Palmas and back. A delightful end to a total of some 37 years in Her Majesty's navy. Some disappointments, some tragedies, some fear, some boredom but never a lack of variety.

FIRST RETIREMENT

When a senior officer leaves the service he is offered the choice of a 'Works and Bricks' course which can be useful when he sets about putting together his property upon retirement, or, for those with aspirations to become an entrepreneur, a six week Business Administration Course to be held at the London Polytechnic. As I was about to enter commerce, had never heard of a margin and a balance sheet was a haze of figures, my new Company insisted that I take the latter. Out of the 42 Generals down to Commanders, only 5% joined the course secure in the knowledge that a job awaited them. Hope I did not look smug but I certainly felt secure.

Retirement from Royal Navy.

Being a new boy with a new department and zero budget, I wondered how on earth I was going to pay my way. The Company was small, overseas selling had never been necessary and money for travel was hardly considered. However, a considerable amount of parcels and equipment had to be despatched to the London area and, coupling the days as a postman, I soon managed to visit every Embassy or High Commission and to meet every Naval Attache or Adviser. At least brochures and my card had found some resting places but still no orders and I was becoming an expensive overhead.

One morning my telephone rang with the news that the Naval Attache in the Kenyan High Commission had been replaced with an Officer who had been Aide De Camp to the President when I was heading his navy. Furthermore he was sitting at his desk with a long list of diving equipment required for the new department just being established. Could I possibly help please? Suddenly I felt like James Dyson with his vacuum cleaners or Richard Branson receiving his first 747 aircraft. My next task was convincing my Lord and Master that the only way to secure this order was a visit to my beloved Mombasa. This was achieved by promising to resign if that £1000 travel expense was not repaid by an order. Fortunately this was awarded to us and I was away.

The bush telegraph is, of course, always up and running and, with what seemed a very short time, our services were wanted, our margins were achieved and the workload increased. Returning from Korea and Japan, and, two days later, Algeria and Tunisia, with my dear wife driving up and down to London Airport like a taxi service, life became hectic. In all, visits were made to the following countries, some many times: Sweden, Norway, Holland, Belgium, France, Germany, Italy, Algeria, Morocco, Tunisia, Libya, Egypt, Oman, Qatar, Dubai, Abu Dhabi, India, Sri Lanka, Bangladesh, Brunei, Hongkong, Singapore, Korea, Japan, Indonesia, South Africa, Kenya, Tanzania, Malawi, Zambia, Bahamas, Barbados, Antigua, Venezuela.

I soon learnt never to say no to a request, and, with a growing reputation of another Steptoe, agreed to provide quotations for equipment I had never even heard of. Go to Nassau in The Bahamas and see the Government band march with British Royal Marine style helmets; fall down a manhole and the name Pearse may appear on the manhole covers in front of your eyes; call in at Algiers and have your yacht life raft serviced by a service station set up from Southampton; sail into Lumut, the home of the Malaysian Navy and witness the large range of Training boats as used in the Royal Naval College Dartmouth; watch the flags unfurl on Independence day in many countries. Actually I did not achieve a sale of sand to Iraq.

As can be imagined, incidents were many, some exciting. Being asked by the stewardess whether a woman could sit on my lap during landing and take-off in a flight between between Dacca and Bangkok (overbooked); leaving the metal flaps belonging to our East African aircraft, on Amsterdam runway; attending a five hour wake of my Agent, (perhaps appropriately named Dr Godlive Epelle), who died in front of me in Ministry of Defence Nigeria; 23 landings and take offs in 21 days in one Far East visit (this time accompanied by my wife); returning from Kuala Lumpur on Monday, back again on Wednesday with Tender Documents lost by the courier and home once more on Thursday. What's jet lag?

After five years of this, it became clear that I required more assistance and duly recruited Commander Peter Neale, a fellow retired naval officer friend of mine, to ease the strain.

Whilst this nomadic and frenetic life continued, The Falklands War had begun and we, in Camper and Nicholsons were busy supplying more and more equipment to commercial vessels being included in the armada. At the same time slight anxieties were running around in my mind.

When a senior officer leaves the service, he is offered a "Dormant Appointment". In the event of an emergency requiring call up, at least he is sure of knowing what his task will be. In my case the dormant appointment was one of convoy commodore. QE2 and CANBERRA would need just that and why not me? Although an exciting thought, my interests lay in my job and it was with some relief that the days passed without a telephone call from 'them upstairs'.

Like most large conglomerates, Crest Nicholson held an annual two day get together of senior executives of all the companies, usually only of Director rank. Whilst in Algiers I was to receive a telex (remember?), asking me to try and return early and report to The Royal Bath Hotel, Bournemouth. Mystified, I managed to achieve this, still none the wiser. Nothing was to be explained until dinner when, during speeches, I was presented with The Chief Executive's cup for outstanding achievement over the past year. Always nice to know that one's efforts have been noted!

This was not to be the last surprise when, shortly after the dinner, I was called to God's office and invited to become Sales Director of the Company. This would include all sales and also responsibility for personnel. The only thing I knew about being a Director was that, in the event of things going wrong, Directors can be held responsible and could even go to prison. Having been mollified on this and encouraged by my wife, I accepted the following day.

Still more was to come when, at 0830 one morning, my phone rang and there was the Chief Executive of the large Engineering group, Fairey Marine, inviting me to pay him a visit but without giving any reason. Fairey Marine was a company in Hamble, not only retail but also manufacturing aluminium boats for use around the world including USA. They were in need of a Sales Director to cement it all together. Interesting to be head hunted and an attractive proposition, but, at the age of 58 and the need to move house, the idea did not appeal and I refused the offer. However all was not lost and, after admitting to my chief executive that there had been shenanigans behind his back, my salary received a considerable boost.

Traditionally, British shipyards had built many of the warships for emerging nations. And when the time came for fitting out and provision of loose equipment, the redoubtable Royal Navy Stores Department stepped into the breach. Now however, more and more orders were being placed in foreign shipyards.

Blohm and Voss shipyard in Germany was building a large Corvette for the Nigerian navy and my curious mind wondered who was to equip the vessel. Accordingly an inquisitive visit was paid to the yard and, sure enough, it became apparent this was still in the 'too difficult folder'. Furthermore the Nigerian Navy was very British in its outlook and training, and the German shipyard had no idea of what the Nigerians may expect. And so, a rather relieved shipyard asked us whether we would be prepared to make a list of all items which we considered a corvette should carry. We were prepared to put forward this list but at considerable cost to them. However, in the event of our securing the order for the equipment, this money would be deducted from the total outlay. No, not blackmail, just business.

Even with my first fairly newly joined colleague, it was clear that we simply did not have the capacity to undertake this considerable task and so another retired officer, Lieutenant Commander Peter Moens, was invited to join us for a two month stint at a fairly meagre four figure sum. In the event he stayed more than seven years!

Armed with the list he produced, he travelled to the shipyard and returned with the sizeable order. Not only did the list include safety and navigation equipment but also sheets and bedding, stationery forms, and toilet paper and toffees for the canteen. More about this later.

The smaller shipyards in the Far East had an abundance of manpower on very low pay and it was not unusual for one man to be responsible for sourcing, obtaining quotations and buying, only one, or at the most two, items. Good for employment statistics but very extravagant. Following our success with the German shipyard, further visits were made to smaller shipyards, mostly in the east, to educate them on the attractions of packages of equipment.

Not only could discounts could be given but the convenience of all equipment arriving at the same time as one package, was tidy and comforting in the extreme. And so began the next phase and before long we were supplying an Italian shipyard with entire packages for four large minesweepers being built for Malaysia, and a similar arrangement for a small Malaysian yard building a large number of patrol craft for the Malaysian Police.

In 1981, the British Government joined up with British Airways to initiate a competition to find a National Salesman of the Year. It was decided that Camper and Nicholsons Marine Equipment Ltd should enter this competition and, as Sales Director, my name was to be put forward. I am not aware of the large number of entries but the final dozen were to be interviewed by a panel headed by Lord Forte, of Trusthouse Forte Ltd. My interview seemed to pass without drama but I was told later, that what had impressed (or astounded?) Lord Forte, was a British Company who could export toilet rolls and chocolate to Germany and, also to supply flags to flutter on flagpoles outside his hotels!

Salesman of the year award.

United Biscuits and Camper and Nicholsons Marine Equipment were pronounced joint runners-up, with the winner being a gentleman in Re-Insurance who spent his life in Concorde rushing around the world, and who was then presented, as a prize, with a further flight in Concorde. I wonder why he won – MIAOW? Runner up prize being a certificate presented personally by the Board of Trade Minister. Not quite the same thing!

At 60 years of age, the strain was beginning to tell, and I realised the time had come to slow down and so I retired. However I now had a plethora of contacts around the world and for another four or five years I continued to travel, helping two UK, one Belgian and one Italian companies to meet the appropriate people in areas in which they were trying to obtain sales. But this was more at my leisure and when I wished, and my wife and I were able to enjoy several holidays in places which we would not, otherwise, be able to afford.

Never before had I achieved selling on a golf course. Asked to make up a fourball, I enquired of my partner, his line of business, and to which he replied that he was 'in motor cycle spares', but being a keen golfer, was branching out into golf equipment, having been awarded exclusive distribution of a new Scottish golf club manufacturer. Informing him that, the following day, I was going to the Far East, he asked if I would like to investigate the market there. As I was now freelance and my air fare paid for, I agreed. Two days after my arrival in Singapore, the gentleman was overjoyed to receive an order from Singapore for a large number of sets of golfclubs, a good number of golf bags and other small equipment. Four weeks later I was in Kenya and another order appeared. This was continued here and there, finally, resulting in a freebie golf set and bag. All in all at 7% commission, a nice little earner!

BOLDRE CHURCH

The ashes of my Mother and father are placed in the Remembrance Garden of St John The Baptist Church in Boldre, Lymington. It is not surprising that, although living outside the bounds, we decided to apply to join the electoral role of that church.

HMS HOOD

By May 1941 the continuous onslaught of the U-Boats in the Atlantic, was beginning to tell. Aerial reconnaissance showed that the German battleship BISMARCK, accompanied by the heavy cruiser PRINCE EUGEN, had left her home port and was passing into the Atlantic. Once this had been achieved, with no radar then being available, she would have been difficult to detect and her destructive force amongst the convoys would, in all probability, have brought Britain to her knees. Accordingly, and in spite of appalling risks this would bring elsewhere, every available ship and aircraft was despatched to intercept and destroy this force. Amongst this vast armada was the undoubted pride and joy of the Royal Navy, the battlecruiser HMS HOOD, a formidable vessel of 48,000 tons.

On 24th May 1941, HOOD, PRINCE OF WALES and supporting vessels engaged the enemy force. HOOD was hit and a fire started on the upper deck. Shortly afterwards she blew up with a massive explosion – the exact cause of which is unresolved to this day – and she disappeared beneath the waves in a matter of a few minutes. With her went 1415 Officers and Men and only three survived – probably the largest loss of life ever known from a British man-of-war.

Embarked in HOOD was Vice Admiral Lancelot Holland. He, and his family, were regular worshippers at the small, over 900 year old parish church of St John The Baptist at Boldre in the New Forest. They had already presented the pair of inner doors to the church in memory of their son who died in 1936, and Mrs Holland felt there should be some lasting recognition of those who were lost in HOOD. From this idea, developed the HOOD Association and a continuing relationship with the church.

In the HOOD corner are; the white ensign flying over the Book of Remembrance, beautifully produced in calligraphy; a signed picture of the vessel by the famous marine artist Montague Dawson; a glass case containing the models of HOOD and BISMARCK, used in the Channel 4 documentary 'The Battle of The Denmark Straits'; and a tampion from one of HOOD's guns. In the porch are two Vice Admiral's lanterns, originally the property of the Holland family; a stained glass window of St Nicholas, the patron saint of sailors; framed photographs of the ship; and two oak benches engraved with the ship's crest of a Cornish Chough.

Throughout the church, runners and kneelers predict HOOD – it is a veritable naval museum. Among guest preachers at the annual service have been the Chaplain of the Fleet in 1994 and 1997, and the Archdeacon for the Royal Navy in 1998. In 2003, the then Vicar writes; 'every year on the Sunday closest to 24th May, a Service is held in our church to commemorate the loss of HOOD. Attended by relatives of those lost and of others in accompanying vessels, by children and grandchildren and others from all parts of the world, the small church with 328 seats, is packed, many standing, with over 380 souls. As a 'post war baby', I thought it would be hard for me to prepare and enter into the service with enough feeling and sensitivity to meet the needs and expectations of the hundreds who gather year by year. That feeling was dispelled three years ago when I led the service for the first time and stood next to Lieutenant Ted Briggs (sole remaining survivor of the three) as he read the words of the Commemoration. I began to feel just a little of the loss experienced by so many of the congregation and I, and so many of my generation, need to be reminded of the sacrifice made for our freedom. And there needs to be a place of focus for this memory – this is the continuing role of St John's Boldre'.

The Vicar continues, 'for how long should we continue this act of commemoration? This is the cry of some around me – both those of my age and, more often, those who still have permanent memories of the sinking. This is the question prompted by the winding up of the D Day Landing association. Perhaps it is better to stop something in a positive manner than let it simply fizzle out – but perhaps not... having said all this, the present desire to meet together and remember the lost, far outweighs the voice of cessation and so St John's will continue to host the Commemoration for the foreseeable future, and do so proudly, and, I hope, with quiet dignity. I count it a privilege to help, and be with those who want to remember, and I pray for a healing of those memories – and peace – both personal and universal'.

Thirteen years ago, the then Vicar intimated that the pre-planning, organising and running of the HOOD service as it is called, was encroaching on his other important duties as Vicar, and asked whether I would be prepared to take it on. This I did and from which I have received great satisfaction.

As I write, our current Vicar, who has a delightful sense of humour, decreed that, after thirteen years of helping to organise this service, I should be rewarded with an invitation to be guest preacher at the service on 13th May 2007. Lecturing

The Preacher.

and after dinner speaking, yes, but never, so far, preaching. I suppose, at my age, I may be excused a few gaffes and so, let's give it a try. Yet again my brain was stretched to the limit.

With my wife having served on the Parochial Church Council and with other duties of custodianship of the burial register, intercessions, lesson reading, car parking and church cleaning coming our way, we have been kept busy but this lovely place has always given us great peace and solace.

Now well into our eighties, we take comfort and pleasure in our children and grandchildren, but with time to reminisce and dream. Tragedies, dramas and disappointments yes, but the good times were many. I am a contented man.

SERMON AT HMS HOOD SERVICE, ST JOHN THE BAPTIST CHURCH BOLDRE, 13 MAY 2007

One of my tasks while helping the Vicar to organise this annual HOOD service each year, is to arrange for guest Preachers.

As some of these are of considerable age like me, I have sleepless nights just before each service in fear and dread that flu or a sudden hip operation will disallow the appearance of the good person. In sailor's parlance I took a seamanlike precaution and jotted down a few notes and these have been locked away securely for some years.

At one of my meetings with Camilla, I mentioned this to her. Her response was to reward me for my 13 or so years service by suggesting that if no guest preacher had been arranged for 2007, then these notes should be taken out of the filing cabinet and dusted down and I should be the guest preacher and, in view of my growing decrepitude, this had better be now rather than later. Our Vicar has a keen sense of humour!

Shortly after the loss of HOOD, as an 18 year old I was on my way to join another battleship, WARSPITE, where I was to spend nearly three formative years of my life as the lowest form of animal life, namely a Midshipman. As you came into the church you may have seen the magnificent 9 foot model of WARSPITE, built by Colin Vass, who so kindly presented the models of HOOD and BISMARCK placed in HOOD corner. May I extend my thanks to Colin for bringing it down today although the model is not yet quite complete. It has brought back many memories to me. Naively I (and God Bless her, my Mother) imagined that the mighty battleship must be the safest bit of metal afloat. But already BARHAM, PRINCE OF WALES, ROYAL OAK, REPULSE, HOOD had all gone to the bottom within the first two and a half years of the war and with this realisation my morale took a dent. And my fears were to be justified later when WARSPITE was brought to her knees by Hitler's bombers at the Allied landings at Salerno in Italy.

Although the majority of the congregation here today know the tragic story by heart, there may be a few who wonder why, every year and more than sixty years later, there is this quiet and thoughtful service here in Boldre. Of course, and it goes without saying, the appalling and crushing fact of 1415 sailors being lost in a matter of seconds, needs to be remembered. But we all recognise that throughout the war and at other times, sadly there were many other losses and occurrences equally hard to bear.

You will have seen the poignant pictures on TV of HOOD's ship's bell lying on the seabed. Shortly after the programme, a letter appeared in the Times suggesting that the bell should be raised and placed alongside the Tomb of The Unknown Warrior in Westminster Abbey. My reply was published the next day saying that if the bell was to be raised then the right and proper place for its safekeeping was here in St John's Church. Personally, and I know this a view shared by the Association, I believe it should remain where it is.

Every one of what we call 'the great disasters', is a compound of tens or hundreds or thousands of individual sufferings; and are not the real sufferers

Models of HMS Warspite and HMS Hood.

Model of HMS Hood.

the individuals who die or who are wounded, together with those who mourn them or who worry for their wounds? Oh yes, there can be great empathy in the emotions of those who are not thus involved, and the greater or more dramatic the disaster, the more widespread the empathy; and of course those who die in the service of their country, deserve the individual gratitude of their countrymen as well as national recognition of the greatness of their sacrifice.

Just before the 2005 HOOD service here, I received a letter (sadly one of several – all bemoaning the fact that their age disallowed their attendance), from Vice Admiral Sir Louis Le Bailly. I am afraid, once again, he has expressed his sadness at not being able to be here today, but has asked me to deliver this message: "That the Boldre St Johns Church Council and the Vicar and Commander Tony Pearse between them keep this annual service going and that so many of you come, makes me bitterly regret my fractured vertebrae keeps me almost housebound: especially as my Mother was one of the Holland clan. With my best wishes I must couple those particularly who keep the Association flourishing and of course our President, Lieutenant Briggs. I knew his signal deck well. There was a float controlled very hot water tank on the mast for the Admiral's cabin and without fail, as Briggs may recall, it always rained boiling water whenever a signal exercise was happening. And it was I who took the can!" With this letter he enclosed a short article which he had written and which was printed in the Salisbury Review in early spring last year. If I may I will read a little of it:

Model of DKM Bismarck.

"The 24th of May is a special day for me. My ship, HMS NAIAD – heavily down by the bows from three hits and 180 near misses in a hectic four hour battle with Hitler's air force, was limping back to Alexandria. We had buried our dead during the night. Then, just as we came to our buoy in the harbour and the hospital barges came alongside for our wounded, we heard that HMS HOOD had been sunk. I had served in her, aged just 17, for over a year, rejoining four year later, and after 30 months service, went to war in her. Of the 1415 lost I had known 300 of the engine room crew, all lost, and probably a couple of a hundred others. The sudden destruction of my first naval home, leaving only three survivors, was a knockout blow.

Ten months later, I found myself swimming in a choppy sea, on a dark night, as NAIAD sank stern first to the seabed. There was lots of jabbering and cries for help as we tried to get those who could not swim or were burnt, on to the few rafts. And then Leading Stoker Davies, a Welshman with a lovely voice, started to sing Abide With Me as he had learnt the hymn in his Methodist chapel in the Rhondda. Most joined in and the last line 'In life, in death, O Lord abide in me' seemed rather appropriate swimming in 600 feet of water 25 miles from the shore. The task force – less its Admiral, now in the water with us, had sped on its way. As Davies ended, an extraordinary hush ensued. Was it, I have always wondered, 'the peace of God which passeth all understanding?'

And then suddenly HMS JERVIS appeared, by a miracle of navigation for we had no lights. There were shouts to 'hurry up' for the German submarine was still in the vicinity. So, swimming madly, we pushed the rafts to the jumping nets over JERVIS' side. And when, towards the last of us, Davies was helped up them, his great heart gave out and he died.

It has never seemed to matter to me to which Christian church one belongs. Twenty years ago Solzenitzhyn, that writer about Stalin's gulags, where 40 million lives were ended, speaking in London on seeing the empty pews asked: "What happens to society when people have forgotten God?" He knew a cruel Empire which explicitly denied the freedoms to which we are used. Where the State is sovereign there is no place for religion. Only private faith can challenge."

I would now like to address myself to those who have been to sea or who are still serving, and even to those about to follow this calling. Being at sea, a long way from home – in the Pacific Ocean or The Antarctic for instance, can be a lonely and frustrating experience. The presence of one's fellow men only two feet away, the constant noise of generators and the continuous and irritating movement of the ship, can test oneself to the limit.

Once a week, on Sundays, the pipe goes "Clear Lower Deck, Hands to Church" and for 45 glorious minutes peace and calm reigns. It is the moment for reflection, and, for some, prayer. Prayer on the messdecks is never easy and can be open to ridicule, but at church on a windy day on deck, no one knows or bothers, as to whom is passing the time under duress or who is having deeper thoughts. But ALL are having a moment of peace.

We all have differing ideas as to the value or need to go to church. Whatever other reasons there may be, for me, the very fact of being in church brings a feeling of peace and quiet and remoteness from the day to day hassle. This feeling of peace and calm was brought home to me even more when I attended, almost 25 years ago to the day, a meeting of The Society of Friends or Quakers as they are more commonly known and who hold their meetings in silence. I suppose, and indeed am sure, it reminds me sublimely of those few minutes on the quarterdeck. Perhaps some of you feel the same emotions.

We are told that congregations are declining. Some who do not go to church claim they are good Christians and thus have no need to go to church. We are good Christians and are here in church and know that both go together.

When you are in church you not only feel the peace but you also cannot get away from the word of peace. There is the peace of just being there. At

66

Morning Prayer the second collect begins "Oh God, thou art the author of peace and the lover of concord". At the Eucharist we sing "Glory to God on high and on earth, peace, goodwill towards men", and you are then enjoined by the Vicar to wish peace on all around you. And, finally, almost the last words Camilla will say to us today will begin "The peace of God which passeth all understanding".

When you sit beside your children, grandchildren, great grandchildren or friends, relating to them all your memories and experiences, tell them also about the lovely day you had today. Tell them how it brought back the memories of those 45 minutes on Sundays at sea. Example is everything in leadership and most children wish to emulate their elders. Equally there are many, more grown up, who are only looking to be shown the way. If you explain this simple emotion to them and suggest that a little peace might be welcome after a week of chores, late buses, infuriating employers, stubborn parents, endless hassle and sometimes, bullying, then who knows, the next time you go to experience that peace in church, you may have brought along a follower.

At the time of Epiphany, four months ago, our Vicar reminded us that that was the time of focussing on the mission of the church in reaching others by "showing" Jesus as the saviour of all people. She challenged each and everyone of us to show the way to at least one. And what better way, as I have just explained could there be of meeting this challenge?

And so let us now, on this day of remembrance, think of those names that are on the Book of Remembrance over there in the HOOD corner. And listen to the message which they must be leaving us, as they lie in the cold waters of the ocean deep.

"Here dead we lie because we did not choose,
To live and shame the land from which we sprung.
Life, to be sure is nothing much to lose,
But young men think it is, and we were young".

I have talked about peace – so desirable, but so elusive. The nations of the world seem to be unable to find it. But we, as individuals can, if only peace of mind, and that is a very worthwhile aim in life.

A poem by Geoffrey Weedon, himself a Quaker, but which encapsulates the feeling of peace in this place:

"Breathe in the quiet purpose of this place
Through outward stillness, seek a calm within.
Here we can find forgiveness and forgive;
Here feel the healing miracle begin.

Breathe out the busy world, the teeming mind,
The follies, fears and failures of the week:
Breathe out contention, pettiness and pride,
And wait in trust for "that of God" to speak.

Breathe in communion, friend with quiet friend.
Each drawing closer in this timeless hour;
As all our different needs and gifts are drawn
To the one source of comfort, love and power.

Breathe out at last, to God, the heart's full thanks
That we have seen this vision, known this grace;
Renewed through love, let us that love extend
Through all our daily life beyond this place."

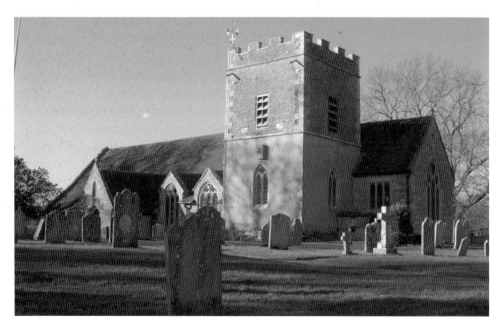

Boldre Church.